Wiltshire's Lost Railways

by
Peter Dale

**Woodborough Station on the
Berks & Hants Extension Railway.**

ACKNOWLEDGEMENTS

I would like to thank my father who, unwittingly, started my interest in this hobby and Ken Jones, a long-standing friend who introduced me to this project.

The publishers wish to thank John Alsop for contributing most of the photographs in this book and Neville Stead for contributing the photograph on page 19.

Rushey Platt Station, 9 September 1961. It had closed fifty-six years earlier.

INTRODUCTION

Wiltshire is largely a rural county, said to have more sheep than people. Salisbury Plain lies in the south-eastern part of it and at the end of the nineteenth century army developments there had a large effect on the railways and their traffic.

Wiltshire was dominated by the Great Western Railway. The first public railway in the county was part of the GWR main line which opened from Faringdon Road (Challow) to Wootton Bassett Road (Hay Lane) on 17 December 1840. The first section of the GWR line to Gloucester and Cheltenham opened from Swindon to Cirencester on 31 May 1841. At the beginning of the twentieth century the Patney and Chirton to Westbury section was built as part of the direct West of England main line and a little later the Badminton line opened, providing a fast route to the Severn tunnel and South Wales. In a way Wiltshire could even be thought of as the heart of the GWR as Swindon was where Great Western engines were made. The decision to build the locomotive works there was made in October 1840. An agreement was made to build the works, refreshment rooms at the station and 300 cottages, which formed the basis of New Swindon. To avoid the expense of building the station the company agreed that the contractor should build it at his own expense, in return for a ninety-nine year lease of the refreshment rooms (which did not cater for third class passengers) and an agreement that all trains would stop at Swindon for ten minutes. This delay was only removed in 1895 after the company paid £100,000 and bought out the lease and stock. The works and village were enlarged several times and now part of the works is a museum to the GWR.

However, the GWR was not the only railway at Swindon. The interloper was the Midland & South Western Junction Railway, which provided a north–south cross-country route between the Midland Railway at Cheltenham and the London & South Western Railway at Andover. This was a gallant little railway that maintained its independence in spite of financial troubles and the hostility of the GWR until it became part of that company in the grouping of 1923.

The LSWR West of England main line ran through the southern part of the county and had a branch largely associated with the military.

It is worth adding a word of explanation here about the grouping for non-railway enthusiasts. Many of the railways in Britain were built by small companies, sometimes with the backing of a larger company. In the years leading up to 1923 there was a process of consolidation by which smaller companies amalgamated or were absorbed by larger ones, but in 1922 there were still well over 100 different companies in Britain. In 1923 all but a few minor companies were grouped into four larger concerns by Act of Parliament. They were: Great Western Railway (which continued in an enlarged form), Southern Railway (which included the LSWR), London Midland & Scottish Railway (LMS – which included the Midland) and the London & North Eastern Railway (LNER). These four companies continued until they were all nationalised into British Railways in 1948.

In an age dominated by road transport it is amazing to think that in 1908 the railways employed over 600,000 people and consumed over eight million tons of coal annually. It is hoped that this book will revive memories of Wiltshire's railways and perhaps encourage some to look again at our railway heritage.

Lavington Station was on the new short route to the West Country and opened in October 1900.

Amesbury & Military Camp Light Railway

			Stations closed	Date
Passenger service withdrawn	30 June 1952		Newton Toney *	30 June 1952
Distance	5.8 miles		Amesbury	30 June 1952
Company	London & South Western Railway		Bulford LSW **	30 June 1952
			Bulford Camp ***	30 June 1952

Newton Tony Station.

* Renamed Newton Tony in October 1903.   ** So-called to distinguish it from Bulford Great Eastern.   *** This was a private station for military use.

In the 1890s Salisbury Plain was being developed for military use and the London & South Western Railway obtained a Light Railway Order in 1898 for the building of a line to Amesbury to serve the army camps of the area. The line opened from a junction with the LSWR main line at Newton Toney Junction on 2 June 1902. Although built under a Light Railway Order, the line was substantially constructed with 87lb/yd rails and there were a number of cuttings and embankments. Amesbury (which is close to Stonehenge) was provided with large platforms and loading docks for troops and horses, Bulford New Camp being about one and a half miles from there. In August 1904 another junction with the main line was made at Amesbury Junction, enabling trains to run onto the line from the Salisbury direction and passenger trains were then normally worked to and from Salisbury. The Bulford Extension Order was granted in 1903 and on 1 June 1906 the line opened for passenger traffic to Bulford and for military traffic to Bulford Camp.

Amesbury Station.

During the First World War a network of lines was built from a junction north of Amesbury extending westwards into the Plain to various military camps with such charming names as Druid's Lodge and Fargo Plantation. These lines were worked by the Railway Operating Department of the Railway Engineers until about 1923 when they were lifted. At first the weekday service consisted of six passenger trains and one goods train with no trains on Sunday. By 1922 there were still six daily trains with one in each direction on Sundays. The service had dwindled to one daily train immediately before the cessation of passenger services. Goods traffic continued until 1963.

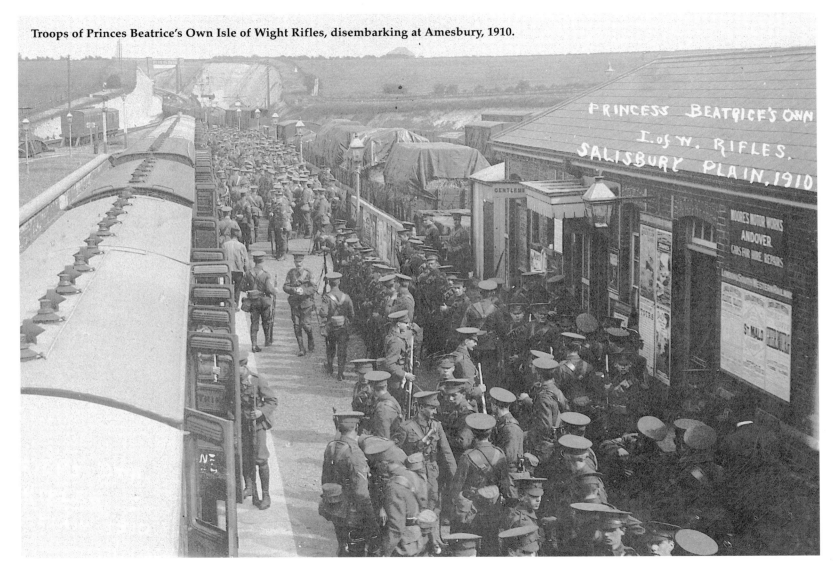

Troops of Princes Beatrice's Own Isle of Wight Rifles, disembarking at Amesbury, 1910.

Chippenham – Calne

Passenger service withdrawn	20 September 1965	*Stations closed*	*Date*
Distance	5.3 miles	Stanley Bridge Halt	20 September 1965
Company	Calne Railway	Black Dog Halt *	20 September 1965
		Calne	20 September 1965

Stanley Bridge Halt. Note the spelling 'Halte' which the GWR used in some places with the introduction of the railmotor service.

* Built as a private station to serve Bowood House.

The signs and the early motorbus at Calne Station are evocative of another era.

The Calne Railway obtained its Act in May 1860. The line was opened as a broad gauge line for goods on 29 October and for passengers on 3 November 1863 and was worked by the Great Western Railway. It was converted to standard gauge over the weekend of 16 and 17 August 1874 and was absorbed by the GWR in 1892. In 1863 there were five daily trains in each direction, but by the 1950s there were fourteen trains taking about fifteen minutes for the journey.

Not all the branch trains originated from Chippenham as some started their journeys in Bristol or Westbury. Railmotors ran the services for many years and they were replaced by autotrains. The line had considerable traffic in the form of special passenger vans carrying the bacon, sausages and other goods of 'Harris's Wiltshire Sausages' from Calne all over the country. Although it was reported that traffic was still rising in the 1950s closure was recommended under the Beeching plan, goods traffic going first in November 1964.

Dauntsey – Malmesbury

Passenger service withdrawn	10 September 1951	*Stations closed*	*Date*
Distance	6.5 miles	Great Somerford Halt *	17 July 1933
Company	Malmesbury Railway	Malmesbury	10 September 1951

Malmesbury Station.

* Known as Great Somerford until 22 May 1922.

The Malmesbury Railway was incorporated in 1872. The Great Western Railway subscribed half of the capital and from its opening in December 1877 worked the line from a junction with the GWR at Dauntsey on the main line between Wootton Bassett and Chippenham. It was absorbed by the GWR in 1880. Malmesbury had appeared in 1864 in the plans of the Wiltshire & Gloucestershire Railway which was to have been worked by the Midland Railway and would have given that company a route to Salisbury. However, a territorial agreement between the GWR and the Midland made that impossible and the scheme was dropped. The branch ran uneventfully until 1903 when the GWR Badminton line was opened, passing over the branch just north of Great Somerford, to provide a shorter route from Wootton Bassett to the Severn Tunnel. At the time of construction of the new line a temporary connection was put in, but it was not until 1933 that a connecting link was laid in from the Badminton line west of Little Somerford to a point on the branch south of Kingsmead Crossing. It was intended that the new link would come into use in February 1933, but there was a legal hold-up as permission to abandon the section south of Kingsmead Crossing to Dauntsey had not been obtained and the new link wasn't used until 17 July 1933 when that section was closed. The line was thus shortened to 3.75 miles. Throughout the 1920s and '30s the line was worked by a 517 class tank and three four-wheel coaches and there was a service of seven trains a day each way, some of them mixed, taking about twenty minutes for the journey. After the new link was put in more modern coaches were provided and there were nine return trains daily. After closure to passengers freight traffic continued until November 1962.

Devizes line

Passenger service withdrawn	18 April 1966	*Stations closed*	*Date*
Distance	Holt Junction – Devizes: 8.2 miles	Pans Lane Halt *	18 April 1966
	Devizes – Hungerford: 24.5 miles	Devizes	18 April 1966
Company	Wiltshire, Somerset & Weymouth Railway/	Bromham & Rowde Halt	18 April 1966
	Berks & Hants Extension Railway	Seend	18 April 1966
		Semington Halt	18 April 1966

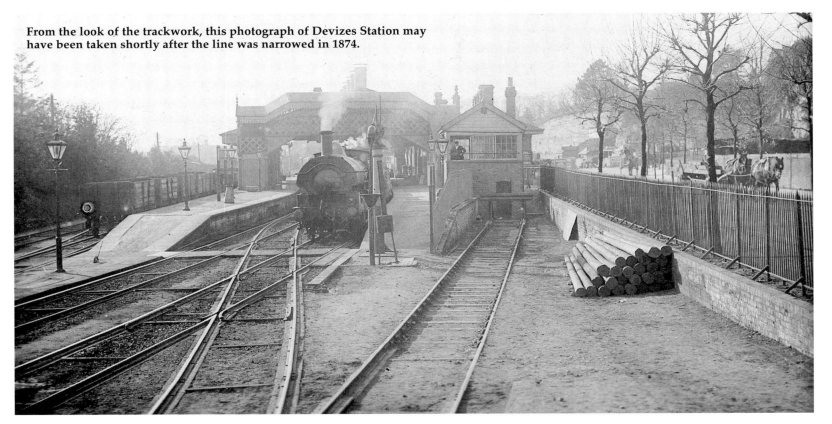

From the look of the trackwork, this photograph of Devizes Station may have been taken shortly after the line was narrowed in 1874.

* Known as Pans Lane Bridge Halt when it opened in March 1929.

Bromham & Rowde Halt.

Devizes was on the Kennet & Avon Canal, but was not on the Great Western Railway main line nor among the proposed branches. A number of proposals for branches to Devizes were made by the Wiltshire, Somerset & Weymouth Railway and the line from Holt Junction was built, but only after delays which forced the GWR (which took over the WS&WR in 1850) to get an extension of time to their Act in 1854. The broad gauge line opened on 1 July 1857, about a week earlier than expected, and complaints were voiced locally that there had been no opportunity to organise the normal celebrations. There were no intermediate stations between Trowbridge and Devizes. At first there were up to seven daily trains and even four on Sundays, but by September there was, as usual, no Sunday service. In 1846 proposals were made to extend the Berks & Hants Railway from Hungerford to Westbury. This did not please the denizens of Devizes as they were to be on another branch line, but in the event the B&HER opened its main line to Devizes on 11 November 1862. The line from Hungerford to Holt Junction was narrowed over the weekend of 28 June 1874 and in 1882 the GWR, which had always worked the line, took over the B&HER. When the Patney to Westbury section of the GWR direct West of England main line opened to passengers on 1 October 1900 the Devizes line was again relegated to branch line status. Nonetheless, the line had through trains as well as a local service and in 1936 many services were diverted onto the line due to settlement of a bridge on the main line between Patney and Lavington.

Ludgershall – Tidworth *

Passenger service withdrawn	19 September 1955
Distance	2.2 miles
Company	Midland & South Western Junction Railway

Stations closed	Date
Brimstone Bottom **	Workmen's station open only during line construction
Tidworth	19 September 1955

In 1900, as part of the development of the army's facilities on Salisbury Plain, a new camp was being built at Tidworth. The Midland & South Western Junction Railway approached the War Department and the line to the camp was built on War Department land under an agreement of November that year. It opened for military manoeuvre traffic on 8 July 1901. The line opened for War Department goods traffic in May 1902 and a public passenger service began on 1 October 1902. It was worked from the outset by the M&SWJR. The intermediate stop at Brimstone Bottom was a private siding (where there was also a temporary village) from where Mr Lovatt, the contractor for the construction of the barracks, conveyed his workers to and from Tidworth using his own trains. The line saw considerable amounts of military traffic and at one time the receipts at Tidworth were greater than those of all other M&SWJR stations combined. After closure to public traffic the War Department continued to run trains until total closure on 31 July 1963.

* The station on this line that was in Hampshire was Tidworth Camp, closed on 19 September 1955. ** A private station for workmen.

Midland & South Western Junction Railway

Passenger service withdrawn	11 September 1961
Distance	Red Post Junction (Andover) – Andoversford: 59.5 miles
Company	Midland & South Western Junction Railway

Stations closed	Date
Ludgershall	11 September 1961
Collingbourne Kingston Halt	11 September 1961
Collingbourne	11 September 1961
Grafton & Burbage	11 September 1961
Savernake High Level	15 September 1958

Ludgershall Station.

Midland & South Western Junction Railway * (continued)

Stations closed	Date	Stations closed	Date
Marlborough Low Level	11 September 1961	Rushey Platt **	1 October 1905
Ogbourne	11 September 1961	Moredon Platform	28 September 1924
Chiseldon Camp Halt	11 September 1961	Blunsdon	28 September 1924
Chiseldon	11 September 1961	Cricklade	11 September 1961
Swindon Town	11 September 1961		

Marlborough Low Level Station.

* The stations on this line that were in Gloucestershire were Cerney & Ashton Keyes, Cirencester, Foss Cross,   ** This station replaced an earlier station in March 1885.
Chedworth Halt, Withington, and Andoversford & Dowdeswell. The station in Hampshire was Weyhill.

CHISELDON

The Midland & South Western Junction Railway followed in the footsteps of earlier schemes to link Manchester and Southampton which had been strenuously opposed by the Great Western Railway. Although they were now connected to the GWR by the Marlborough Railway, the people of Marlborough wanted a connection with Swindon and Southampton. In July 1873 an Act, which was passed unopposed, was obtained for the Swindon, Marlborough & Andover Railway. The line was to be built in two parts, the northern section from the GWR at Swindon to the GWR station at Marlborough, and the southern section from Wolfhall Bridge (Savernake) to a junction on the LSWR West of England main line west of Andover Junction. The gap between these sections was covered by running powers over the Marlborough line and the Berks & Hants Extension Railway. Before the line was opened the plans at Marlborough were changed so that a viaduct was replaced by a long curve which made the intended end-on junction with the Marlborough Railway no longer feasible. The junction was instead placed a third of a mile south of the terminus which meant that the SM&AR had to provide a separate station at Marlborough.

Trial trains, which carried passengers free of charge, ran for about a month before the opening of the northern section to fare-paying passengers on 26 July 1881. There was a delay in completing the junction with the GWR at Swindon and after it was passed by the Board of Trade in October 1881 traffic did not begin until February the following year. By this time the mood of the GWR had changed as the Swindon & Cheltenham Extension Railway had been authorised and the spectre of competition to the GWR's own north-south route loomed again. Inspection of the southern section took place in March 1882 and the arrangements at Savernake were found severely wanting, having been put in place many years earlier. Despite this the section from Grafton to Andover opened on 1 May 1882, but trains did not run through from Swindon to Andover until February 1883. In the meantime work had been proceeding on the S&CER which would give the SM&A an independent route to Cheltenham. The GWR was obstructive, trying to stop the S&CER crossing its Cheltenham and Great Western Union line south of Blunsdon. In this case the appeals went right up to the House of Lords, but the GWR lost the day and the line was opened from Swindon to Cirencester on 18 December 1883.

A GWR Prairie Tank at Swindon Town Station, 16 September 1952.

The SM&A and S&CER merged to form the Midland & South Western Junction Railway in June 1884 and the new company, in a dire financial position, went into receivership in December. The position was so bad that the builder of the rolling stock threatened to repossess it and a night watchman was employed to prevent that happening. Sam Fay became general manager in 1892 and the company came out of receivership in 1897, experience which stood him in good stead when he moved to another impoverished concern, the Great Central Railway. Services steadily improved with through coaches from Birmingham, Bradford, Derby, Leeds, Liverpool and Sheffield running through to Southampton. They reached their height in 1914 with an express from Birmingham and one from Manchester. The M&SWJR became part of the GWR at the grouping, but the GWR continued to run a through coach to Liverpool. After nationalisation there was a rundown of services until there was only one through train a day by the end of 1958. A preservation group with headquarters at Blunsdon, the Swindon & Cricklade Railway, are working to reopen part of the line.

Salisbury & Dorset Junction Railway *

Passenger service withdrawn	4 May 1964	*Stations closed*	*Date*
Distance	19 miles	Downton	4 May 1964
Company	Salisbury & Dorset Junction Railway		

This train approaching Downton Station has just entered the loop.

This line was authorised in 1861 and opened on 20 December 1866 to link Salisbury with the Dorset coast. It was single track with passing loops at the four original intermediate stations (Daggons Road did not open until January 1876) and ran from Alderbury Junction, on the Salisbury to Romsey line, to West Moors on the Southampton & Dorchester Railway. It was worked by the London & South Western Railway from the outset and later leased by that company for £1,600 per annum. It was absorbed by the LSWR in January 1883. During the 1920s there were six trains daily between Salisbury and Bournemouth, with one on Sundays.

* The stations on this line that were in Hampshire were Breamore and Fordingbridge. The stations in Dorset were Verwood and Daggons Road.

LSWR coaches at Downton Station. These had a two-tone livery of salmon pink on their upper panels and dark brown on the lower ones.

Savernake – Marlborough

Passenger service withdrawn	6 March 1933	*Stations closed*	*Date*
Distance	5.6 miles	Marlborough (High Level) *	6 March 1933
Company	Marlborough Railway		

* Known as Marlborough until 1 July 1924.

The Marlborough Railway was promoted in 1860 to build a line from the Berks & Hants Extension Railway at Savernake. This first proposal was opposed by the Great Western Railway as the promoters were considering an extension to the Andover & Redbridge Railway which revived the GWR's fears of a north–south competing route across its territory. The proposal was reintroduced to Parliament in the following session and passed having gained GWR approval, a promise from it to subscribe £10,000 towards the cost and to lease the line when it was finished. The broad gauge line opened to traffic on 14 April 1864. The initial service was five daily return trains until 26 June 1874 when the line was closed for gauge conversion, reopening on 1 July. The GWR absorbed the Marlborough company in 1896.

The Swindon, Marlborough & Andover Railway was incorporated in 1873 and planned to build two separate sections of line that would be united by means of running powers over the Marlborough line and a short section of the B&HER. The GWR was compelled to make many improvements at Savernake for the SM&A and it was not until February 1883 that trains commenced running between Swindon and Andover. It is said that the GWR's employees delayed the other company's trains at times by such tactics as prolonging the ticket inspection at Savernake until a GWR train was due and then allowing this to proceed and thus occupy the line. Another ploy was to hold trains at Marlborough Junction while the staff were fetched from Savernake, five miles away. In 1898 an independent line, the Marlborough & Grafton Railway, was opened to connect the two sections of what had by now become the Midland & South Western Junction Railway and these troublesome tactics ceased. In 1933 the M&SW line was singled and the GWR branch was diverted to that route south of Marlborough tunnel, resulting in two single lines running through one tunnel. At this time the High Level station was closed to passengers, all passenger traffic going to the Low Level station, but it remained open to goods until May 1964.

Swindon – Highworth

Passenger service withdrawn	2 March 1953	*Stations closed*	*Date*
Distance	Highworth Junction – Highworth: 5.6 miles	Stratton	2 March 1953
Company	Swindon & Highworth Light Railway	Stanton	2 March 1953
		Hannington	2 March 1953
		Highworth	2 March 1953

Hannington Station. Note the light railway aspect of the station building.

This train at Highworth Station appears to be worked by a 517 class tank.

This line was promoted by the townspeople of Highworth to link the town with nearby Swindon and the Swindon & Highworth Light Railway received its Act in June 1875. Great difficulty was experienced raising the capital for the line and after three years only £12,000 of the authorised £21,000 had been subscribed. The Great Western Railway was approached, but despite enthusing about the line's prospects no cash was forthcoming. Construction began after a contractor was found who would take the remaining shares in part payment. Not until March 1881 was the line ready for inspection by the Board of Trade. However, Colonel Yolland, the inspector, found the line unsafe to be opened to the public. The directors showed their lack of confidence in the line's engineer, Mr A.C. Pain, who was also engineer to the Culm Valley line and the Southwold Railway. They also dug their heels in and stubbornly refused to give any promise to make good the line's shortcomings and the Board of Trade sent regular notices forbidding opening. Another approach was made to the GWR and in September 1881 they offered £16,000, which the S&HLR had little option but to accept. The GWR took over in August 1882 and made the required improvements so that the line opened on 9 May 1883. The initial service consisted of five daily return trains. In later years railway staff trains were a feature of the line, leaving Highworth for Swindon in the morning and returning again in late afternoon. 14xx series auto tanks normally worked the line during the 1950s and, being a light railway, there was always a 25 m.p.h. speed limit. After the end of passenger services the railway staff trains and a daily goods train continued until final closure in August 1962.

Closed passenger stations on lines still open to passengers

Line/service	London & South Western Railway: West of England main line	Stations closed	Date
		Wilton South *	7 March 1966
		Dinton	7 March 1966
Stations closed	Date	Semley	7 March 1966
Porton	9 September 1968		

Porton Station.

London & South Western Railway Station. Porton.

* Originally known as Wilton (LSWR); renamed on 16 September 1949.

Dinton Station.

Dinton Station.

Semley Station.

Line/service	London & South Western Railway: Salisbury – Eastleigh (Bishopstoke)	Stations closed	Date
		Salisbury Milford *	2 May 1859

* Opened on 1 March 1847, this was the first station in Salisbury.

Line/service	Great Western Railway: Thingley Junction – Bradford Junction *	Stations closed	Date
		Beanacre Halt	7 February 1955
		Broughton Gifford Halt	7 February 1955
Stations closed	Date	Holt Junction	18 April 1966
Lacock Halt	18 April 1966	Staverton Halt	18 April 1966

The unusual combination of a railmotor, van and an 0-6-0ST at Lacock Halt.

* Melksham Station also closed on this line on 18 April 1966, but was reopened on 13 May 1985.

The junction for the Devizes line was at Holt Junction Station.
The train is headed by a GWR 4-4-0.

Stations closed	Date
Heytesbury	19 September 1955
Codford	19 September 1955
Stockton Crossing *	after July 1915

Stations closed	Date
Wylye	19 September 1955
Langford	October 1857
Wishford	19 September 1955
Wilton North **	19 September 1955
Salisbury ***	12 September 1932

The rear vehicle of this train at Heytesbury Station seems to have been added to the normal train – perhaps it was a saloon for a special party.

* Opened after 1907, this was a private station for the use of workmen.
** Known as Wilton (GW) until 26 September 1949.

*** After this date GWR trains used the Southern Railway's station at Salisbury.

Codford Station.

Codford Station.

Wylye Station.

Wishford Station.

Wilton North Station, August 1921. The train is headed by a GWR 4-4-0.

Line/service	Great Western Railway: West of England main line	Stations closed	Date
		Manningford Halt	18 April 1966
		Woodborough	18 April 1966
Stations closed	*Date*	Patney & Chirton **	18 April 1966
Savernake for Marlborough *	18 April 1966	Lavington	18 April 1966
Wootton Rivers Halt	18 April 1966	Edington & Bratton	3 November 1952

Woodborough Station.

* Originally named Savernake Low Level; renamed on 11 September 1961.   ** Originally named Patney Bridge.

Patney & Chirton Station was the eastern junction for the Devizes line.

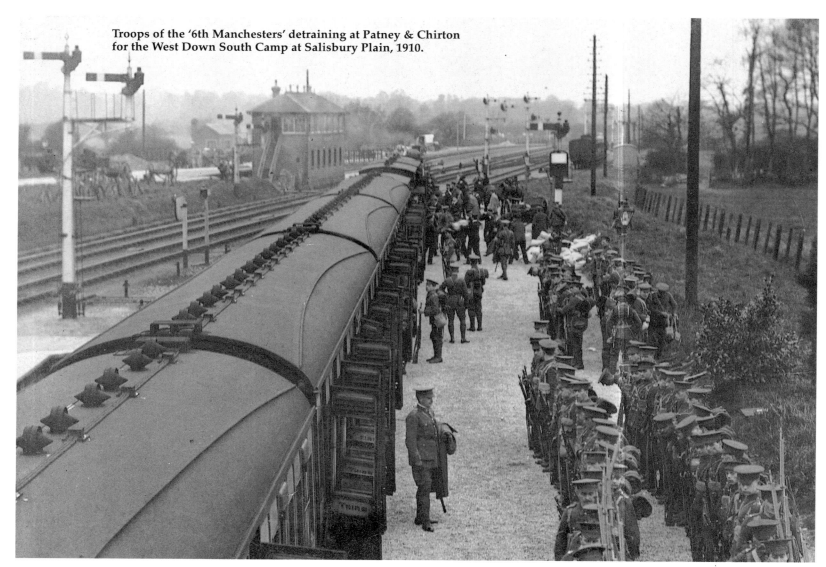

Troops of the '6th Manchesters' detraining at Patney & Chirton for the West Down South Camp at Salisbury Plain, 1910.

Lavington Station.

Line/service	Great Western Railway: Swindon & Bath main line		Stations closed	Date
			Dauntsey	4 January 1965
			Christian Malford Halt	4 January 1965
Stations closed		Date	Corsham	4 January 1965
Stratton Park Halt		7 December 1964	Box (Mill Lane Halt)	4 January 1965
Wootton Bassett Road *		30 July 1841	Box	4 January 1965
Wootton Bassett Junction **		4 January 1965		

Wootton Bassett Station was the junction for the South Wales line through Badminton.

* This was a temporary terminus, situated at Hay Lane, which opened on 17 December 1840 during construction of the GWR.

** Originally named Wootton Bassett; renamed on 1 July 1903.

The branch train for Malmsebury at Dauntsey Station.

Corsham Station.

G.W.R. Station.
CORSHAM. 539.

Stations closed	*Date*
Purton	2 November 1964

Stations closed	*Date*
Minety & Ashton Keynes *	2 November 1964
Oaksey Halt	2 November 1964

Purton Station.

* Known as Minety until 18 August 1905.

Line/service	**Great Western Railway: Badminton line**	*Stations closed*	*Date*
		Little Somerford	3 April 1961
Stations closed	*Date*	Hullavington	3 April 1961
Brinkworth	3 April 1961		

Hullavington Station.